Sermons in Stone

Books by Mel Ellis

Flight of the White Wolf
Ironhead
Sad Song of the Coyote
Wild Goose, Brother Goose
Softly Roars the Lion
Run, Rainey, Run
This Mysterious River
Caribou Crossing
The Wild Runners
Peg Leg Pete
No Man For Murder
Sidewalk Indian

INSPIRATIONAL
FABLES FOR TODAY

Sermons
in Stone

by MEL ELLIS

illustrated by SuZanne

HOLT, RINEHART and WINSTON
New York   Chicago   San Francisco

Published simultaneously in Canada by Holt, Rinehart
and Winston of Canada, Limited.
Library of Congress Cataloging in Publication Data
Ellis, Melvin Richard,   Date
     Sermons in stone.
     I. Title.
PS3555.L615S4   813'.5'4   74-5096
ISBN 0-03-089589-8
Designer: Mary M. Ahern
Printed in the United States of America
First Edition

To each child on leaving home:

You cannot stay forever. It is the way of the world, so you must go. And now I only hope that during the years you were with me, I wrapped your hearts tenderly in the dewy, green leaves of home so they will stay fresh for planting. Then, when the season is right, root yourselves and the years will grow strong dreams.

But if at first you come upon barren soil, know that somewhere there are lush valleys. Know also that come deserts or mountains, lands far or near, whether one flower or wide-flung fields and high forests . . . know that you, too, are of the earth and it will comfort you.

Try for truth, of course, but then if you do not find it, know that it is there in the snail and the earthworm, in the lily and the oak tree, in the stars and moon on ruffled waters.

Then, should you be wearing sackcloth or satin, understand that your origins are as humble as the solitary blade that struggles from a crack to spread grass on concrete; never falter because you are strong as the roots that split the rocks.

And do not grieve. Rather rejoice that you go, because out there are mountain peaks of such grandeur as you have never yet imagined. And be not afraid. The sun is everywhere.

Sweet are the uses of adversity;
Which, like the toad, ugly and venomous,
Wears yet a precious jewel in his head;
And this our life, exempt from public haunt,
Finds tongues in trees, books in the running brooks,
Sermons in stones, and good in every thing.

> *As You Like It*
> William Shakespeare
> Act II, Scene 1, Line 12

Introduction

I would rather prune a tree than a paragraph. To pluck weeds so a row of carrots may stand supremely green against the sun gives me more satisfaction than turning a phrase. If there is joy in having written, there is positive glory in coming each evening to view such progress as my ferns, my fruits have made. If it is satisfying to pick up a book I have written and see my name and feel the cloth, it is nothing compared to the feeling of fulfillment that comes through my fingertips when I touch the leaf on a tree I have planted.

Neither in nuptial bed nor the sometimes glory of a war have I risen to such inspiring heights of life as those that send my spirit soaring across the golden waves of canary grass in fields I have planted. I feel kinship with the earthworm, the white grub, black ant, born there in the loam, and I would sometimes wish I might explore with them the white roots of the dandelion, or travel deep where the taproot spears for water. Ecstasy surrounds me in the rhythm of existence, and the atom of my atom is in the ant, vision of my vision in the flash of the sun.

Why this obsession with the earth? Why this necessity to touch wood, smell resin? Why God there in my violet? My life in the smooth turn of a stone?

Is it because in the fiber of all of us there is the pulse of earth from which we have surely sprung? What other womb except earth, no matter what ephemeral fantasies we, otherwise, spin about our origins? And what matter the catalyst, if from each harvest we keep such seed as guarantees tomorrow? Is this not faith enough that we guard and give and be the true steward?

A bird's wing reflected on a wave. Wind shredding cloud, unfolding flower. Whirlwinding universe of stars. The world in one raindrop. Evening glow in the eye of my beloved. Heaven? After this earth who needs a bonus?

MEL ELLIS

Contents

Sermons in Stone

Most Beautiful Music

A young Reporter was sent to interview a Maestro, just back from serving a prison term for a political crime. Of the Musician, free once again to compose, orchestrate and direct great music, the Reporter asked: "What in your opinion is the most beautiful piece of music in the world?"

The Maestro pondered, rubbed his brow thoughtfully, and looked out toward the horizon.

The eager Reporter pressed on: "While you were imprisoned what did you most want to hear? What would you say was the *most* beautiful music?"

"In all the world?"

"In all the world," the Reporter repeated.

"In all the world the *most* beautiful music," the Maestro said, and now there were tears in his eyes, "is the sound of another voice."

Man's Chances

ONCE upon a tomorrow those great gray whales, which had survived the years of slaughter, swam to the shallows of an ocean bay to call to convention all the animals of the earth. When they were all gathered it was a sight to see: minnows swimming alongside sword-fish, armadillos and tigers, lumbering moose and agile antelopes, elephants, monkeys, giraffes, butterflies.

The Whale asked for order and then called the roll, showing those missing: auk, quagga, passenger pigeon, Falkland wolf . . .

When the Whale had finished reading the long list, a Tortoise moved that a committee be charged with bringing man to account for thinning the ranks of all creatures. Some recommended man be banished from earth, though they didn't know how to accomplish this. Others were for putting him in cages. The discussion became heated. Just as the convention seemed about to dissolve in the acid of their differences, a grizzled gray Opossum asked for the floor.

"Seventy million years ago I walked the earth," he began, "and let me tell you there were giants then. But they are dead, and I am here to tell you they died of their own greatness. We have nothing to do except to wait."

The meeting ended. And then all went back to jungle and mountains, fields and forests, rivers and oceans, plains and deserts—to wait.

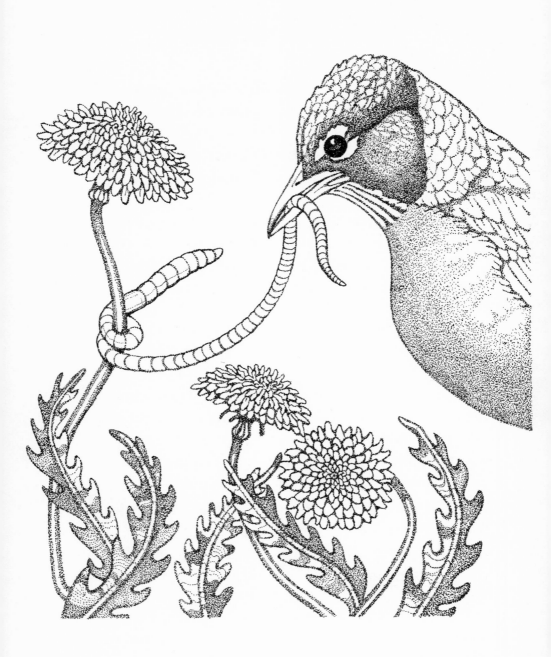

Robin and the Worm

MANY, many years ago on a certain large lawn a Robin was surprised to hear the Earthworm he was about to eat say, "Wait!"

Cocking an eye at the Worm, the Robin said, "Yes?"

"I have a proposition," the Worm said.

"Keep talking."

"If you will eat only my tail and then let me go, I will grow a new tail and give it to you."

The Robin, though skeptical, remembered how arid August can be—the heat made the worms stay deep in the ground.

"Take a chance," the Worm pleaded. "I really can grow a new tail, and I really will come back to give it to you."

So for a time, then, there was a large lawn where not even during the scorching days of August did the robins lack for worm tails, and never during any springtime were earthworms afraid to wander far looking for lovers.

Then one day there came a strange bird, a greedy bird from a faraway place, and he ate an entire worm. Word spread quickly throughout the worm colony.

And so, even to this day, the worms no longer trust the robins but, rather, wait until the sun has set and the birds are asleep before coming from their deep burrows to wind their way across the cool, wet lawn. And that is why, even in other circles, the worms came to be called nightcrawlers and why, on arid August days, robins hop across parched lawns often hungry for the worm tails that were once so plentiful.

The Rainbow Trout

A Rainbow Trout that lived in a crystal-clear creek was captivated nightly by the bright glitter of the stars. Each evening, as soon as it was dark, he would come from his watery hole beneath an undercut bank and, holding fast in the current, wondered how it would be to swim through a black velvet sky so full of shining diamonds.

As the Rainbow Trout grew, so did his obsession. The quiet place where he daily rested among the roots of a leaning cedar tree became intolerable, and he was only happy when he could come out into the current and look up into the night sky.

Still, only looking was never enough, and so, finally determined, Rainbow Trout positioned himself. Then, with a powerful surge, he vaulted from the water and landed high on the bank.

There were seconds then, before oblivion, when Rainbow Trout could look down, and there, right in the watery place from which he had so wanted to escape, were all the stars shining more brightly than he had ever remembered them.

The Lonesome Snowflake

A Lonesome Snowflake, having come to sparkle on the blue spruce bough of an outdoor Christmas tree, fell in love with a brilliant red light on a bough below. While tens of thousands of other snowflakes were happy to love only one another, the Lonesome Snowflake yearned to come close to the red light.

Hours went by, and the night was growing old, and some of the other snowflakes had gone swirling away from the spruce to be embraced by the white banks on the ground. As morning dawned and the Lonesome Snowflake had about given up hope, a breeze suddenly unseated it. Joyously the Lonesome Snowflake began a gentle descent toward the strange one it had come to love.

Even at a distance the Lonesome Snowflake could feel the delicious warmth and, hurried a little by the wind, it came to the bright heat of the red light, and then its indiscreet love turned it into a tear.

Wilderness Wine

WILD grapes in lush clusters on climbing vines, having hung beyond the days of ripeness, fermented and their juices had turned into wilderness wine. A Young Raccoon, smelling the tempting odor, was eager for his first taste. The sweet-sour fruit was not as palatable as a crayfish, though on entering his stomach it spread a welcome warmth all through his body.

Finally surfeited, the Young Coon ambled unsteadily toward a crystal creek where he bent to drink and, in the vagaries of the current, he thought he saw three coons mocking him.

Indignant, the Young Coon dove from the bank to rout the intruders, but the icy water took his breath away so that when he swam to shore and looked again, the strangers had fled.

Then he met an Old Coon and told him how he had chased the raccoons that had been staring up at him from the creek.

The Old Coon glanced in the direction of the wild grapes. "And had you been eating of the grapes?" he asked.

The Young Coon averred that he had, and was in fact going back at this moment to eat again of the purple clusters.

Old Coon grinned. "In that case," he said, "when you go back to the creek you will find the rogues waiting for you."

The Little White Cloud

A Little White Cloud spent each sunny day playing with the wind. Alone in the big blue sky, it could change into such delightful shapes that it brought quick, excited laughter from the earth below. One moment it would be a white swan, the next a sailing ship. Then it might change into a horse with streaming mane, or into a waterfall.

Inevitably, other clouds formed along the western horizon. The Little White Cloud was fascinated. As the western clouds put up towering black peaks and white cliffs, the Little White Cloud, having never seen such majesty, gazed in awe.

"Hurry away with me," the wind said to Little White Cloud, "you can always come back."

But the Little White Cloud said, "No, I too want to grow to be a towering cloud with shining cliffs and black peaks."

"You may have joy or power. You can't have both," the wind said.

The Little White Cloud did not go when the wind left. Amid lightning and thunder the Little White Cloud grew and began to pulse with power. It got bigger and bigger. Finally the sky could only weep at such violence and the magnificent, powerful cloud rained down and disappeared to drain away in the earth's rivers.

An Icy Reflection

KINGFISHER, a blue arrow of a bird, patroled his pond and with raucous, rattling war cry delighted in putting every other feathered thing to flight. So enamored did he become of this power over his watery dominion, that when fall arrived he could not bring himself to leave.

Then when the terns flew south, he dove at them so they hurried beyond his reach. And when warblers, sparkling as winged jewels, skirted the pond en route to warmer climes, he scattered the flocks. And he chased migrating redwings and the tree swallows that swarmed like green raindrops, until the last of the summer birds, a long-legged brown bittern, lumbered by.

Then the Kingfisher's pond froze and he moved up into the area of the creek. When the creek froze, he moved to the springhole. And here even the winter birds did not come and there were plenty of minnows and he should have been happy. But he wasn't.

Then one day when the ice of the creek was casting back the sun's reflection, he was suddenly startled to see a bird below. Overjoyed to find yet another victim, he dove with a war whoop to route the intruder.

In spring, when the other birds returned, they found only the few blue feathers of the Kingfisher who had come face to face with his icy reflection.

Horizons

OF a Young Boy looking out a classroom window the Teacher asked: "And what do you see out there?"

Jerked abruptly out of his reverie, all the Boy could think to say was, "The horizon."

Instead of scolding the Boy for daydreaming, the Teacher asked, "And have you ever walked to the horizon?"

The Boy thought for a moment then said, "No, I am too young."

"Well, someday you will," the Teacher assured her pupil.

At once the Boy was interested, and he asked, "And when I get there, what will I find?"

"When you get there," the Teacher said, "you will discover another horizon—another far beyond."

Then the Boy blurted out, "And if I walk again?"

"Yes, and if you walk again you will know that the second horizon is merely a starting place toward the third."

Disappointed and disenchanted the Boy asked, "Will my life then be one of always losing horizons?"

"No, of always *finding* them," the Teacher answered.

Little Creek

O<small>F</small> all things, Little Creek wanted to be big. However, nothing, not even little creeks, can grow until many other streams have donated their experiences.

And so Little Creek, determined to get big, went charging down the valley where it was joined by other little creeks until it became a mighty river.

Sweeping along it cut faces in rock and moved sand-bars at will, and sometimes surged from its banks to carry homes and farmlands with it.

Finally convinced it was the mightiest of Creation's phenomena, it came hurrying into the anonymity of the sea, and then as its powers were diffused, it wished with all the vigor now spent, that it might be just a little creek bubbling forever between the low beautiful banks of its happy beginnings.

The Turtle and the Horse

HARDLY higher than a kitten, a prehistoric Horse that had been often plagued by drought, wind, rain, and predators came to envy a Turtle that lived in a pool at which it watered.

Often then, the Horse wished it too might bask on a log in the sun, retreat from attack to within a shell, deposit eggs in the earth and forget about caring for its young. And during such wintertimes as finally came upon the earth, the Horse wished that it too might, like the Turtle, sleep away the colder days buried in the mud, taking such oxygen as it needed through the skin around its tail.

But instead the Horse was much vexed by insects, ever plagued by the predacious big cats, and, in order to survive, it had to paw deeper for grass roots during blizzards and to learn to run faster than all its enemies.

And so eons passed and the Horse grew. Then one day the Turtle, still looking exactly as it had millions of years ago, looked up at the now large, swift, strong Horse and said, "I would give anything in my world to be as big and beautiful as you are."

Then the splendid Horse pranced and shaking its mane proudly said, "Then you will finally have to come out of your shell."

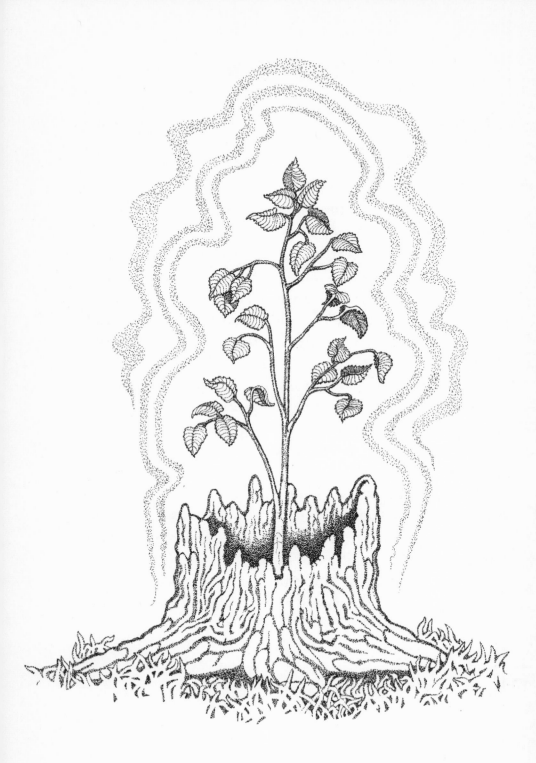

Eternal Life

AN ancient Elm stood tall, looking out across the other trees to see the winding silver ribbon of a creek and the flowers on the hill. It had withstood not only the ravages of time, but all such other assaults that had been made by wind and ice and insects, to become the largest and most noble creation on the horizon.

But now, almost leafless, no orioles came to hang nests from its limbs, and there were only woodpeckers to add insult to injury by boring holes through its bark.

So when its time came it did not go down in some gloriously riotous wind or with a significant crash, but fell slowly in a little puff of dust—no proper salute to such a monarch.

Supine then, with sap still coursing its woody veins, it wondered to what purpose it had lived. Lying there the seasons turned its once-massive trunk into a decaying mound, but before the last thin pulse was extinguished from the final fiber of its life, it felt a quickening as, from its grave, lifted miraculously a green colony of new elms.

Then the ancient Elm, realizing that here burgeoning was the life of some other monarch, knew at last about the dignity of death.

Room for Every Living Thing

ONCE upon a time a Man was given some acres to do with as he pleased, so he dug a pond and stocked trout, which he had to share with the kingfishers. He planted spruce trees too, and the hordes of grackles that came to nest retarded the growth of his trees by perching on and breaking off the tender new leaders.

Not yet deterred, he bought some white lily tubers, duck potatoes, and other beautiful water plants, but the muskrats came and got fat.

Still he persisted, planting wild grapes for each autumn's harvest. But the vines grew as thick around as a man's wrist and, climbing, throttled trees in their clutches.

So the Man sat on the bank of his pond not knowing what to do. He liked kingfishers and grackles and muskrats—but he also wanted his fish and trees and water plants. In the end he did nothing. And nature turned spruce branches skyward to replace the broken spires, grew enough water plants for the muskrats with some left over, produced a surplus of fish, enough for the kingfishers and the Man, strengthened trees so that they rose above the grapevines—established a place and made room for every living thing.

Moving the Pines

WELL taught, the Boy knew where to cut the new growth so the thousands of small white pines in the nursery directed all energy into such boughs and spires as would make each a splendid tree. But for all his pruning, weeding, and cultivating there came a day when the young trees no longer responded to his efforts.

Turning to his Father, the Boy asked, "Why, in spite of everything I do, are the trees not growing?"

"It is time they are moved," the Father replied.

"Moved?" the Boy asked. "But how can that help?"

The Father put an arm around his son's shoulders and said, "When the fingerling becomes a big fish it must leave the creek for the river."

So the Boy, while transplanting the thousands of young pines, grew also and became a man.

At last, when his work was done and the trees were all flourishing, he turned once more to his Father. "And now," he asked, "now that I have transplanted all the trees, what is there for me to do?"

The Father's smile was sad. "Now the trees can take care of themselves," he said. "Now it is your time to find other acres as will accommodate you. It is your time to go."

Pebbles in a Puddle

IT was a bleak alley, an almost hideous place of grimy brick walls, broken pavement, and a scattering of fetid garbage. A night's rain had left dirty puddles in the road, and a lone Derelict walked among them trying to keep his feet dry.

At the first streak of dawn, a Little Girl came to sit beside one of the puddles and then, when the sun rose over the buildings that hemmed in the ugly alley, she tossed a pebble into the puddle.

The Derelict, pausing in his perusal of garbage cans, stood to watch. Intrigued, he finally asked, "And why do you throw pebbles into the puddle?"

"Can't you see?" the Little Girl asked.

"See what?"

"Come closer." The Derelict did. "Now watch."

Then the Little Girl threw another pebble, and the Derelict, his rheumy eyes still clouded with nighttime, leaned forward.

"Watch now," the Little Girl cautioned, "and see how the sun can paint the little waves with silver."

Rubbing his eyes, the Derelict saw the running circles of sun, and they put such a glint even in his old eyes that they were still shining when he walked away.

Adversity

O NCE there were two tiny oaks, hardly high as a squirrel's eye. One stood right on the edge of the prairie. The other, surrounded by water, grew from a bog in a springhole.

Each year then, when the fires came sweeping, the tiny Prairie-Edge Oak lost its few leaves and its small trunk was seared. But, being surrounded by water, the Springhole Oak was spared. Of course the Prairie-Edge Oak became scarred, twisted, and ugly.

"You're a disgrace to the rest of us oaks," the Springhole Oak said, looking over to where the Prairie-Edge Oak stood.

But then came the winter of the rabbits, and after they had eaten all the lush, soft seedlings that are furnished by willows and poplars, they turned in desperation on the two oaks.

But, try as they might, the rabbits could not cut through the layers and layers of scar tissue on the trunk of the Prairie-Edge Oak. So they leaped to the bog where the Springhole Oak stood and, since the little tree had had neither trial or tribulation, it was soft and the rabbits, quickly girdling it, ate the bark.

Then, during the first warm days of spring, while the gnarled Prairie-Edge Oak made the little gains it always made, the Springhole Oak slowly withered of its wounds and finally, since it had never learned about adversity, died.

Rugged as an Oak

"GRANDFATHER?" the Father said to his small son. "He looked like the burr oak, rugged and strong."

"And what will I look like when I grow old?" the Boy asked.

"What do you want to look like?"

The Boy thought awhile and then said, "I'm not sure . . ."

"Walk in the forest and look at the trees. Perhaps then you will be able to decide."

So the Boy walked into the forest. He admired the tall pine, looking down on the other trees. He also liked the way the spruce laid graceful tiers of green boughs all the way to the ground. When he smelled the perfume of the flowering linden, he decided it would be pleasing to go through life surrounded by such a sweet aroma.

But perhaps, he thought, it would be better to be laden with fruits like the wild cherry or plum, or hanging with nuts like the hickory or walnut. Or maybe, after all, it would be glorious to flame like the maple in fall.

In the end then he couldn't decide, and when later he told his father so, the Father replied, "Take the best from each: be as charitable as the plum, as sweet as the linden, as far-seeing as the pine, as well-rounded as the spruce, as brilliant as the maple; and then when you are gone, no matter. People will always say you looked sturdy and strong as an oak."

The Envious Junco

THERE lived a Junco considerably dissatisfied because his tree stood where he could watch through a hen-house window and see a flock of chickens being fed. Then he would fly off to search the byways for weed seeds. Sometimes there were enough, sometimes snow covered the weed seeds and he would be left hungry. Then, with an angry flirt of his tail, he would come back to look with envy upon the warm, fat, comfortable, and complacent hens.

Those days when he was most exasperated, he would fly to the window and flutter his plum-colored wings to see if there wasn't some way to get through the glass so he too could be warm and comfortable.

But there was no way, and so each time he returned to his tree to fluff himself into an indignant ball of feathers and reflect upon such worldly mismanagement.

Each day then, the Little Junco spent more and more time envying the chickens, and less and less time hunting for weed seeds. So he became bedraggled and surely one day would have fallen from his perch and likely perished, except that suddenly the hen house became a hell as the chickens, one by one, were put on the chopping block. Horrified, the Little Junco flew to find another tree, where there was no window of want, and to this day he is glad for weed seeds.

The Monument

An Old Man, having lived an exemplary life in the service of others, had come to his time to die, and so a Friend said: "You will not be forgotten. We have found a tremendous piece of granite to stand as a monument to you so the future generations will remember."

The Old Man shook his head.

"But what then?" the Friend asked.

With effort the Old Man raised himself on an elbow and said: "Monuments are for the dead."

The Friend looked perplexed, but refrained from pointing out that that, in fact, was precisely to the point. Instead, he asked, "But what would you have?"

"I would have you take the monument money and plant a tree, preserve a patch of prairie, create a marsh for the geese."

"But, what about your epitaph?"

The Old Man smiled. Then he said, "If a man leaves a park, a playground, a wild-goose marsh, a tree . . . none will ever have to ask: 'And what did he do?' "

The Mockingbird

THERE was born a bird without a song, and since already hundreds of birds were all singing the praises of each day in their own special way, he could find no new thing to sing about. And so he mimicked his neighbors who, in derision, called him Mockingbird.

Now, since there is hardly any honor in imitation, Mockingbird saddened. But instead of deciding on silence, he became more defiant and vehement until he was ostracized from polite bird society.

As Mockingbird continued to sing other birds' songs from more secluded places of exile, his heart was breaking. One night he awakened to see how the moon had silvered the leaves and turned the forest into a softly shining and beauteous fairyland without one bird to sing its praises.

Unbidden then, a rapturous song was born, and that is why Mockingbird, though a mimic all day, saves his own special rhapsody for our darkest hours.

The Skinny Gray Squirrel

From Barren Land to Fat Country came a Skinny Gray Squirrel and, when he saw such a surplus of corn as spilled in golden piles on the ground, he hurried to the feast. Though there was more than enough, the Fat Country Squirrels drove him away.

So Skinny Gray Squirrel sat beneath his wisp of tail in the tangle of a hawthorn tree, holding his tiny paws to his breast to keep the bare pads from freezing. Sometimes he nibbled a dried-up hawthorn bud, sometimes the bitter bark, but mostly he watched the fat ones gorge themselves.

Then one day another Skinny Gray Squirrel came from Barren Land, and he, too, tried to get corn, but the fat ones also chased him away. So the second Skinny Gray Squirrel joined ranks with the first, but to no avail. They might well have starved, except another Skinny Gray Squirrel joined them, and then another and another.

And so it was the society of Skinny Gray Squirrels grew, and then the fat ones, having grown lethargic and lazy with fine feeding, were no match for the razor-sharp thrusts of the angry, hungry horde. And so now the fat ones watch and grow thin, while the skinny ones eat and grow into Fat Country Squirrels.

Seashells

THE Snail, naked in the beginning, was sad not only because he was so slow that all creatures preyed upon him, but also because he was a drab blob in a world filled with exotically colored creatures. So he conferred with the clam, which was also naked, and with naked conches. Although they practiced, they never increased their rate of locomotion, and felt that they would have to wait out their days in the dark and dreary crannies among the rocks.

Except the Snail would not opt for oblivion. As he inched his way across a stone he noticed the trail of slime that he left behind had gradually hardened into a lusstrous streak.

Instead of wasting his secretions on the stones, he kept them to himself, fashioning a coat and adding layer to layer until he was surrounded by a hard shell of many beautiful colors.

So the word was passed on to the other snails, to the clams, the abalones, the cowries, the chitons—more than fifty thousand of the different kinds of creatures that made up this hapless family.

And now, while death destroys the beauty of all of the other of this world's creatures, these snails and clams and conches—when they are gone—leave behind a testament to their ingenuity, which gives us the beautiful shells cast up by the seas.

The Old Man

A Small Boy, his arms full of books, thought as he crossed a small quadrangle: It must be strange to be old and to sit in such a small park on a cold bench lost in a great coat.

So he turned for a better look at the bewhiskered face beneath the battered cap, and the Old Man saw him and, lifting his head, asked, "Yes?"

"I just thought," the Small Boy stammered, "I wondered . . . do you need . . . you look . . . might I . . . can I help you?"

The Old Man smiled. "You already have," he said.

This Glorious Day

ALWAYS when such things as heaven and the hereafter came up for discussion, the same Little Old Lady left the Senior Citizens Central Park Discussion Group and wandered off into a small coppice through which a brook meandered.

Perplexed, a Ministerial Counselor followed her one day and, from a discreet distance, saw her bend to a flower, run her hand over the rough bark of a tree, finger the curve of a stone, blow gently on a spider's web.

When she had wandered off once more and was again returning from among the trees, the Counselor stopped her to ask, "You keep wandering away. Is something wrong?"

"Well, yes . . ." she answered.

"Can I help?" the Counselor asked.

"You can," she said briskly.

"Tell me how," the Counselor said.

"Stop babbling about the hereafter and sing instead of the glories hereabouts and the beauties of *this day*."

The Winner

A Colt, having waxed strong on good grazing and ample rations of oats, went into training. Every day, after each arduous workout, the now mature Colt was brought for a rubdown into a paddock alongside of Invincible, a gelding who had never lost a race.

While stable boys kneaded the Colt's muscles and sleeked his hide, Invincible lectured the Colt, always ending with the admonition: "Winning isn't everything. It is the *only* thing!"

The Colt went on to race, but never won, and was relegated in disgrace to a riding academy. Here his remorse was tempered when his gentleness made him the preferred mount of small children.

Subsequently Invincible, having grown old, also came to the riding academy. However, when he could not become reconciled to such pedestrian pursuits, and when his obsession to win made him break ranks in the riding formations, he was relegated to pulling the manure spreader.

Then, working knee-deep in steaming manure, all he could think of was the glory days as he gazed out across the fields to where the Colt, now actually an old horse, still led long lines of riders through verdant valleys, up timbered slopes.

Quiet Times

THOUGH he had suddenly grown tall, he was not quite a man yet, and on rainy days he became irritated and impatient. One time his Mother sat beside him where he was watching the rain washing like gently breaking glass across the windowpane.

"We need the rain," she said, "as surely as does the earth."

The Boy raised his eyebrows in a silent question, and she kept talking, "Think of it this way: the sky has lowered the shades so the mind may have time to look inward and to slow the heart that pounds to meet the world's werewolves and windmills."

The Boy looked back out of the window, still fidgety. "Take advantage of the quiet times," she continued. "They close wounds surely as rain closes the gaping cracks of drought. Reflect now. Keep your thoughts quiet as a rain-streaked leaf waiting for a brisker time to twirl."

And so the Boy did, and that is how he learned to wait and watch for the rare gift of those quiet dove-gray days when he could pull in his world and hold it close around him.

I Am Somebody

A Young Philosopher, grown despondent in pondering eternity and infinity, could not see how it would matter that he had ever lived. His despair was further compounded when, on an October afternoon on a high hill, he watched a wide valley below ebb and flow with a million swirling leaves.

He thought: Look at the leaves; nothing but confusion. They swirl and tumble and spin without purpose.

Then the wind quieted, and all the millions of leaves settled to lacquer the land. At once he saw that the word "brown" had so many millions of meanings that there were not enough words to describe them. Right then he knew that not one single "red" was precisely like any other, and that the shades of yellow outnumbered the sands, the stones, the stars.

At last he knew that he mattered. He was as much a part of the mystical magic as the beech, butternut, birch, oak, maple, poplar, and each of the trees that had given its leaves to create the grand mosaic of color below.

The Sparrow's Eye

A Boy, pellet gun in hand, came stealthily through the brush until he was but a few feet from a black-bibbed English Sparrow perched on a branch.

Raising his gun, he sighted it on the sparkling Sparrow's eye, an eye that was as bright as a raindrop in the sun. But the instant he squeezed the trigger the light died, and all the wonders of the world, every precious atom that had made the Sparrow's eye Creation's perfect pearl, faded away.

Gone the Glory

L AST of the velvet having been rubbed from his tines, the Buck Deer lifted his head, his antlers a burnished glory in the setting sun. Then, with the fever of creation now running through his veins, he made his raucous way through the forest, battling other bucks, taking does— and when there were neither, charging even trees and bushes.

Sometimes he slept during the day, but the power that is life so consumed him that he ran the ridges at all hours until even the sated does fled at the sound of his ringing hooves, his crashing antlers. At last, when none would come forth to accept his challenge or to seek his favor, he stood alone, deserted by the herd.

With the coming of the first snow, one antler dropped, and then the other, and by the time the mice and porcupines had come to gnaw at the symbols of his Autumnal Glory, he once again touched noses with fawns as well as the does, and lived in peaceful proximity to all the other bucks.

Backyard Gold

THE world, it seemed, became covered with dandelions. People were furious and broadcast poison sprays and gradually the yellow flowers disappeared from all lawns except one. Here, where the last dandelions bloomed, lived a Man who recognized such attributes in the flower as are common to all Great Things.

These values that the Man appreciated included the dandelions' imperviousness to cold, the burst of yellow sunshine they provided not only in summer but in early spring and late fall; their tenacity, the ability to grow from a crack in a sidewalk, to lay a coin of gold on a gray path. What's more, he made a delicious salad from their tender roots, medicine from their long leaves, and he collected enough blooms to make wine for warming the winter days.

Even his children rejoiced in the dandelion. They made necklaces and other fragile jewelry from the hollow stems, colored their cheeks with the yellow pollen, and, when the dandelion bloom turned to a white head of fluffy seeds, they sent them parachuting on the wind.

In time people forgot their early hatred of the dandelion and became jealous of the Man. It wasn't long before they were standing in line to get dandelion seeds, eager for the gold lodes that would make a treasure of their own backyards.

The Third Skunk

Two young skunks, having come to the same field to probe the sod for grubs, stood eye to eye in a territorial dispute.

BROAD-STRIPED SKUNK: I was here first.

NARROW-STRIPED SKUNK: Oh no you weren't.

BROAD-STRIPED SKUNK: Well, I'm not leaving.

NARROW-STRIPED SKUNK: Neither am I.

BROAD-STRIPED SKUNK: But there aren't enough grubs for both of us.

NARROW-STRIPED SKUNK: Tough on you.

BROAD-STRIPED SKUNK: We'll see about that.

Broad-striped Skunk arched his back, lifted his tail, and then pranced menacingly. Narrow-striped Skunk did likewise.

Around and around they went until a Third Skunk came down the lane. Seeing the two young skunks threatening one another, he said, "Looks to me like you're both cowards."

Whereupon each of the young skunks, disregarding skunk etiquette, loosed a barrage of vile fluid. Then, when the two went stumbling from the field sick and dizzy, the Third Skunk began eating the grubs.

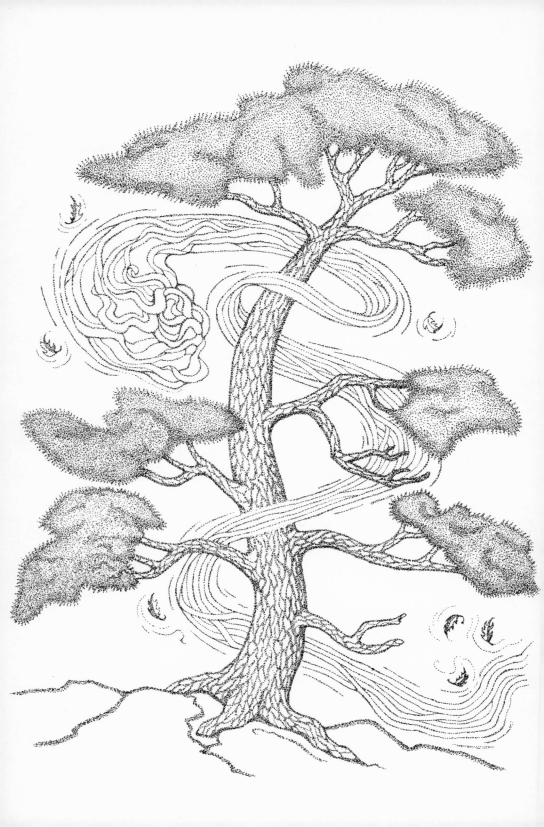

The Singing Wind

INORDINATELY proud of its voice, the Wind howled through the forest. Having blown down a grove of trees, it paused to catch its breath beside a still-standing Pine that asked, "Why did you want to do that? Without us you would be a very monotonous fellow."

"Oh?" said the Wind.

"Yes, without us the best you might ever do is whine, or perhaps roar a little."

"Ridiculous," said the Wind.

"Then go to yonder prairie and let me hear you sing."

And so the Wind went to the prairie where there were no trees and, racing in vain, could indeed only whine and roar a little.

Exhausted it came back and went soughing softly through the Pine. It found the bole of a hickory and blew a high note, and thrumming the end branches of an oak made the muffled thunder of drums. In a spruce it sang a sadder song. Through the hollow of a maple it found a bass note. It sang high and low, sad and joyful songs in many a tree crotch, among a multitude of flaring branches, through leaves of all shapes and needles of many textures.

And then, when it had come at last again to rest beside the Pine, the tree said, "See. Alone you can only make sounds. Together we make music."

Nobody Gets the Moon

THE moon was in the creek and, thinking it might be edible, the Fox wanted it. Except every time he put forth a paw to scoop it out onto the bank, it shattered—broke into a multitude of shining shards.

Exasperated the Fox sat back. A Beaver, who found him pondering the problem, asked, "Something bothering you, Brother?"

"Help me get the moon," the Fox said.

"Nobody gets the moon," the Beaver answered.

The Fox, suspecting the Beaver wanted the moon for himself, showed his teeth and said, "If you know what's healthy for you, you'll help."

So the Beaver dug a ditch to divert the stream. As the water receded, the Fox poised to pounce and, when the moon was trapped in a last little puddle, he dived on it.

Then when he had extricated himself from the mud, he heard the Beaver chortle, "Look, it's over here."

Which indeed it was, beaming now, in the new ditch the Beaver had dug.

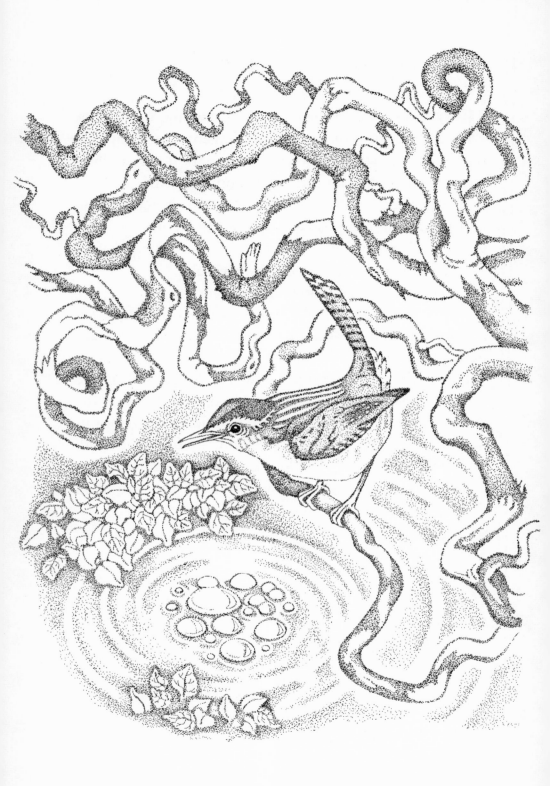

Constant Spring

A broken wing tip had rendered Tiny Wren incapable of sustained flight, and the best he could do was flit—from reed to bush to bough to branch. When the summer birds left, he remained behind. And, when a brisk northeast wind whipped snow through the marsh, he sat fluffed among the cattails, trapped by winter. Thus it was that he began his search. Coming upon a reed below which a muskrat looked up from a hole in the ice, the Wren asked, "And where can I find Spring?"

When the muskrat only laughed, he flitted on, asking a gloomy crow, a mink, a possum—the answer was always the same: "You'll never find Spring around here."

Still, in his heart, which was hardly larger than an apple seed, Tiny Wren knew he would find Spring. Though the storm was severe enough to put eagles down, Tiny Wren went on—tail jerking, head bobbing—until he did come to a warmer place.

Where a creek-bank spruce had toppled to put up a shield of writhing roots, a spring bubbled and boiled. The constant water, never varying from its deep-ground temperature of forty-eight degrees, warmed the air around it a little so here watercress was still green, insects still lived—and in this miniature oasis there was food and shelter sufficient to succor Tiny Wren, who had never doubted that surely somewhere he would find Spring.

The Twin Maples

Twin maple seeds twirling to earth fell within a few feet of each other, one on a fertile lawn, the other into the crack of a concrete sidewalk.

In that first year, though the Lawn Maple thrust out roots to raise an eight-inch sapling, Sidewalk Maple had trouble staying alive.

In the second year, being well fed and well watered, Lawn Maple jumped an incredible three feet, whereas Sidewalk Maple, pale and wan, had grown barely three inches.

In the third year the roots of the Sidewalk Maple finally widened the concrete crack and came to earth. Still, being beneath the sidewalk, the earth was not well watered and never fertilized, and so instead of growing a leafy crown, as had Lawn Maple, Sidewalk Maple put all its efforts into pushing its roots down to a deep underground vein of water.

Then came the hot summer of no rain and, when Lawn Maple withered and lost its leaves in July, Sidewalk Maple stayed brilliantly green. And in fall when Lawn Maple, who had never grown deep roots, died, Sidewalk Maple turned a glorious and triumphant red.

The Morning Glory

ONCE, when the world was young, there was a field filled with a multitude of beautiful flowers, which at that time bloomed only so long as the sun shone. If a cloud came they closed their blossoms, and on dull days the field was a dreary place.

Then, there gradually evolved one, a blue bell-shaped bloom with an ivory chalice and pearly veins, which by noon of each day had to close its petals because the sun was too hot for it. The more brazen flowers belittled the delicate one, and sardonically called it Morning Glory.

One noontime towering clouds came out of the west to darken the field. Though all the flowers hid their faces, the bell-shaped blue blossoms widened with a happy smile. A man seeing this bright visage on such a dark day brought it home from the field and gave it an honored place. So now Morning Glory arches on trellises over the doorways of many homes to brighten man's more dreary days.

The Foolish Donkey

A furry Foolish Little Donkey was so fascinated by a certain White Stallion that he convinced himself that if he could but jump and prance and arch his tail and shake his mane like the Stallion, he might indeed become a horse himself.

So when he was not being loaded down with sticks for the cooking fires of his Peasant Master, he would go cavorting across the Mexican countryside, leaping over low cactus with hooves coming high in a fancy prance.

Children of the little village laughed and began to call him "the donkey who thinks he is a horse." But so obsessed was the Foolish Little Donkey that he could ignore the children's laughter, but he did so resent hauling firewood that he would often go cantering off to scatter the load.

At first his Peasant Master, a patient man, tried gently to show the Foolish Little Donkey that he was being ridiculous by trying to be something he could never be. But then, patience worn thin, the Peasant Master picked up one of the sticks and brought it down with a resounding thwack across the Foolish Little Donkey's flank.

In surprise and pain the Foolish Little Donkey threw back his head and brayed. Ever after the little furry one hid the truth from foolish men. He would let his long ears flop and with mincing step would haul wood back to the village. Yet all the while the truth was that in his heart he was still a horse.

Happenstance?

A tiny Wisconsin sticktight, often called Bootjack, attached itself to a passing horse's fetlock. There it stayed until it came to the hill where it was left in the road as the horse stomped, only to be hoisted, almost at once, by a passing dog.

The dog brought Bootjack into a home and over to the arm of a chair where the sticktight quickly clung to the jacket of a man who, shortly thereafter, took a plane to New York City.

Bootjack next lost its grip in a Madison Avenue Publisher's office, and when a young lady bent to pick up a paper clip, it clug to her hair.

While packaging some page proofs for a Wisconsin writer, the young lady's hair fell across her face and, when she brushed it back, Bootjack fell among the galleys.

So Bootjack came back to Wisconsin, and this morning I took it between a forefinger and a thumb and carried it back to that damp place from which it had started the trip.

The Singing Brook

PRETTY YOUNG GIRL: How old are you, Small Brook?

SMALL BROOK: Old enough to court you with a wink of my bright water.

PRETTY GIRL: Don't tease. Tell me truly. How old are you?

SMALL BROOK: I am old as my rippling laughter, old as my sparkling eye.

PRETTY GIRL: But when were you born?

SMALL BROOK: Many, many, many years ago.

PRETTY GIRL: Then you are very, very, very old.

SMALL BROOK: I am old as the Old Mountain, young as Spring's First Flower.

PRETTY GIRL: If you are so very old, how can you still be so very young?

SMALL BROOK: Because nothing, not even the cold, gray ice of Winter, can silence my song.

The Moon Moth

A large, pale green, soft-winged Luna Moth, whose ancestors had navigated for eons on the light of the stars, had for days now been obsessed with the desire to leave the forest and fly to the glowing horizon that marked the City of a Million Suns.

Not even the aroma of a Male Luna, tantalizing on the soft nighttime breeze, was as compelling as the necessity to fly to where the bright lights beckoned.

Lifting above the treetops, the Luna Moth was carried swiftly by the summery wind until she floated high above the glittering city. Twin moons decorating each of her long-tailed wings glowed brilliantly, as Luna Moth pitched down the sky to be enveloped by the City's glitter.

Overwhelmed, the Luna Moth wing-danced hysterically around one of the bright stars, coming closer on each revolution until she felt the heat. Abandoning caution, she closed her wings to embrace the light and fell away sizzling.

Then, on crippled wings she would have returned to the forest, but bewildered she flew until she fell because here, in the City of a Million Suns, there were no stars to guide on.

Seven Wonders of the World

GEOGRAPHY students, having traveled around the earth by book, were asked at semester's end to list what each considered the Seven Wonders of the World.

Though there was some disagreement, the following garnered the most votes: Egypt's Great Pyramid, the Taj Mahal, Grand Canyon, Panama Canal, Empire State Building, St. Peter's Basilica, and the Great Wall of China.

While assembling the votes the Teacher noted that one student, a Quiet Girl, had not turned in a paper.

"Did you have trouble?" the Teacher inquired of the Quiet Girl.

"A little," the Quiet Girl replied, "I couldn't quite make up my mind because there were so many."

"Well, tell us what you have, and maybe we can help," the Teacher suggested.

Hesitantly the Quiet Girl got to her feet. Then she began, "I think the Seven Wonders of the World are to touch and to taste, to see and to hear . . ." she hesitated, "and then to *run* and to *laugh* and to *love*."

This Precious Promise

A small barefoot Girl in a pair of patched jeans dug with a stick in a narrow strip of clay between the sidewalk and the curb, which fronted on the dilapidated house in which she lived. Then she glanced at the seed packet in her hand, at the picture of the bright promise of vivid pink poppies and, loosening the infertile soil, made a bed for seeds.

Carefully she watered the plot and soon tiny green spears appeared. A Man, in passing, paused to say, "They'll die. Nothing pretty ever grows from such filth as we've got around here."

And it seemed the Man prophesied correctly, because one by one the green spears wilted until only a single plant struggled for life.

The Girl redoubled her efforts, watering the single plant regularly, shading it from the too-hot sun, washing the leaves free of grime, loosening the soil around the roots, guarding the plant against careless feet.

Then one morning a bud opened, and by noon the seed had kept its promise and a pink poppy was a spot of brilliance. All afternoon people passing paused to smile at the Poppy. And only the Man who had prophesied failure smiled, not at the Poppy but at the Girl, because he knew that even in this unlikely place, *she* was the precious promise.

Mind Over Matter

IN a time long past a Little Snake slithered up out of the grass to coil on a flat stone and reflect on how he might catch birds that flew before he could strike, mice that ran more swiftly than he could crawl, and frogs that jumped before he could catch them.

Because he hadn't been born with legs or wings, and was destined to crawl forever on his belly, he often went hungry. Creatures he would prey upon were even contemptuous of his shortcomings and would let him come quite close before fleeing.

So the Little Snake slithered down off the warm rock and retired to a dark cave to meditate. For days he went without food and only when his many ribs were showing, and even his elastic skin was beginning to sag, did he come out armed with a powerful if invisible advantage: the knowledge that the mind could dominate.

So today when he sways his head rhythmically and flicks his forked tongue, the sparrow waits paralyzed, the mouse stands mesmerized, the frog pauses hypnotized —never victims of any special Little Snake magic, but prisoners of fear, hostages of mind over matter.

Impatient Tulip

OF a hundred tulip bulbs buried in the black loam, there was one not willing to wait patiently and, when Winter frosts heaved the garden, it levered its way upward so as to be ready for a quick, green start at the first thrust of Spring sunshine.

Then when a warming rain softened the earth it came spearing out into the world vibrant with the excitement of being first.

Beneath and all around, the other tulip bulbs waited patiently in the dark as the First Tulip made a bud so it might flower.

But even great talent needs timing, and impatience is as much a reason as any why many beautiful things perish unsung. Just as the bud was about to open into a flame of color, Winter came back.

The frost blighted the First Tulip's green spears, shriveled its unfolding bud, and left it lying limp. Then when Spring finally came, it tried to rise but the crisp cold had taken its toll, and the stricken flower had neither the strength nor the roots left to come to proper glory. And so it died, while the other ninety-nine tulips put forth fat, full spears of green that were quickly topped by flowers of many colors.

Enemies?

A Boy, searching for wild strawberries in deep grass, strayed into a patch of nettles and came away with a blistered skin.

"It is an evil plant," he told his Mother, as she bathed the rash.

"Because it tried to protect itself?" the Mother asked.

In Conclusion

DAUGHTER: Now that I have read your fables I am disappointed because you gave no space to the new morality.

FATHER: Well, there are many, many things I did not touch on. As for morality, almost every generation claims a new morality. It is but a vagary.

DAUGHTER: I'm not quite sure I understand.

FATHER: Consider the climbing vines. Honeysuckle, for instance, always twines clockwise, to its right. Jasmine always twines counterclockwise, to its left. Nothing can make either do otherwise. Yet there is a Chilean twining plant, *Scyphanthus elegans*, which will start turning in one direction, making a couple of loops around its support, and then go back the other way, reversing itself every couple of loops or so.

DAUGHTER: Well it would seem the Chilean's is the more interesting way to climb.

FATHER: More interesting perhaps, but not a very tidy system.

DAUGHTER: I still don't get the point.

FATHER: The point is that no matter how vines climb, whether to the left or to the right, or both ways, each is always seeking the same thing.

DAUGHTER: And that is?

FATHER: Light.

Born and raised in central Wisconsin, Mel Ellis has always been an outdoorsman. His knowledge of wildlife and conservation has inspired many of his works, including *Sad Song of the Coyote, Softly Roars the Lion, Ironhead, Wild Goose, Brother Goose, Run, Rainey, Run, Caribou Crossing, This Mysterious River, Flight of the White Wolf*, for which he won the Sequoyah Children's Book Award in 1974, and *Peg Leg Pete*, for which he won the Council of Wisconsin Writers Award in 1974. Mr. Ellis presently resides with his wife and family on a chain of little lakes in southern Wisconsin.

SuZanne, Mel Ellis's daughter, studied at Layton School of Art and the Milwaukee Area Technical College. She illustrates the author's nationally syndicated column, "The Good Earth Crusade." Horsewoman and amateur naturalist, she grew up close to the earth, at Little Lakes in southern Wisconsin, and now lives with her photographer husband, Richard Cherba, in Milwaukee.